GA

CENGA

Drama for Students, Volume 21

Project Editor: Anne Marie Hacht

Editorial: Michelle Kazensky, Ira Mark Milne, Timothy Sisler **Rights Acquisition and Management**: Margaret Abendroth, Edna Hedblad, Jacqueline Key, Mari Masalin-Cooper **Manufacturing**: Rhonda Williams

Imaging: Lezlie Light, Mike Logusz, Kelly A. Quin **Product Design**: Pamela A. E. Galbreath

Product Manager: Meggin Condino

© 2005 Gale, a part of the Cengage Learning Inc.

Cengage and Burst Logo are trademarks and Gale is a registered trademark used herein under license.

For more information, contact
Gale, an imprint of Cengage Learning
27500 Drake Rd.
Farmington Hills, MI 48331-3535
Or you can visit our Internet site at

http://www.gale.com

ALL RIGHTS RESERVED
No part of this work covered by the copyright hereon may be reproduced or used in any form or by any means—graphic, electronic, or mechanical, including photocopying, recording, taping, Web distribution, or information storage retrieval systems—without the written permission of the publisher.

For permission to use material from this product, submit your request via Web at http://www.gale-edit.com/permissions, or you may download our Permissions Request form and submit your request by fax or mail to: *Permissions Department*
Gale, an imprint of Cengage Learning
27500 Drake Rd.
Farmington Hills, MI 48331-3535
Permissions Hotline:
248-699-8006 or 800-877-4253, ext. 8006
Fax: 248-699-8074 or 800-762-4058

Since this page cannot legibly accommodate all copyright notices, the acknowledgments constitute an extension of the copyright notice.

While every effort has been made to ensure the reliability of the information presented in this publication, Gale, an imprint of Cengage Learning does not guarantee the accuracy of the data contained herein. Gale, an imprint of Cengage Learning accepts no payment for listing; and inclusion in the publication of any organization, agency, institution, publication, service, or individual does not imply endorsement of the editors or publisher. Errors brought to the attention of the publisher and verified to the satisfaction of the publisher will be corrected in future editions.

ISBN 0-7876-6818-4
ISSN 1094-9232

Printed in the United States of America
10 9 8 7 6 5 4 3 2 1

The Spanish Tragedy

Thomas Kyd

1592

Introduction

The Spanish Tragedy (New York: W. W. Norton, revised edition, 1989), a play by English dramatist Thomas Kyd, was written between 1582 and 1592, when the first known performance took place. Kyd was a popular dramatist in his day, although most of his plays have been lost. *The Spanish Tragedy* is one of very few extant plays that can with certainty be attributed to him. The play is important not only for its own merits but also because it is the first example of a revenge tragedy, a type of play that was to become extremely popular on the Elizabethan stage during the last decade of the sixteenth century and beyond. The most famous of all revenge tragedies is Shakespeare's *Hamlet,* and some of the plot devices in *The Spanish Tragedy*, such as the protagonist's hesitation in carrying out his revenge, are echoed in Shakespeare's play.

Kyd based *The Spanish Tragedy* on the tragedies written by the Roman playwright Seneca, whose plays focused on murder and revenge. The emphasis was on a malignant fate that led inevitably to a bloody and horrific catastrophe.

Although *The Spanish Tragedy* is not performed in the early 2000s, its intricate plot, full of intrigue and even containing comic incidents, its swift-moving and sensational action, the questions it poses about the nature of justice and retribution, and the well-developed character of the revenger, Hieronimo, make it a rewarding play to read.

The exact date on which Thomas Kyd was born is unknown, but he was baptized on November 6, 1558, at a church in London. His father, Francis Kyd, was a successful scrivener, that is, a man who copied documents. Kyd's father was sufficiently well off to send his son to the Merchant Taylors' School, which had a reputation for high academic standards. Kyd entered the Merchant Taylors' School when he was seven years old, in 1565. The poet Edmund Spenser was also a student there at the time. Kyd may have remained at Merchant Taylors for eight to ten years, although his date of departure is unrecorded.

After leaving school, Kyd was probably apprenticed to his father, although this cannot be established beyond doubt. By 1583, he had begun writing plays for the company of actors known as the Queen's Company. Kyd wrote for this company until 1587, although none of his plays has survived. In 1587 or 1588, Kyd entered the service of a lord, possibly the earl of Sussex, as a secretary or tutor. In 1588, he published a translation of Tasso's *Padre di Famiglia,* under the title *The Householder's Philosophy. The Spanish Tragedy*, the play on which Kyd's fame rests, was written between 1582 and 1592, probably before 1587. It was the first example of an Elizabethan revenge tragedy and enjoyed great popularity during Kyd's lifetime and beyond. What other plays Kyd wrote is a matter of conjecture. He may have written *Soliman and Perseda*, and many scholars argue that he wrote an early version of *Hamlet,* although no trace of such a play exists.

In 1591, Kyd shared his lodgings with the dramatist Christopher Marlowe. In 1593, Kyd was arrested and questioned about whether he had any role in writing pamphlets that incited violence against foreigners in London, who were being blamed for outbreaks of the plague and a rise in unemployment. There is no evidence that Kyd did anything wrong; he was under suspicion only because of his association with Marlowe, who was notorious for his atheism. Marlowe was also arrested but was quickly released (and killed in a tavern brawl twelve days later). Kyd was not so fortunate in his dealings with the authorities. Heretical writings were found at his lodgings, but Kyd claimed they belonged to Marlowe. He was subjected to torture during his brief period of imprisonment, but he was not convicted of any crime.

After his release, Kyd wrote *Cornelia*, an adaptation of a play by the French playwright Robert Garnier. It was published in 1594. In his dedication, Kyd commented about the bitter times and great suffering he had endured.

Kyd died later that year, at the age of thirty-six. He was buried on August 15, 1594.

Plot Summary

Act 1

The Spanish Tragedy begins with the ghost of Andrea, a Spanish nobleman, and the personified abstraction of Revenge. Andrea explains that he was killed in battle against the Portuguese. This deprived him of his secret love, Bel-Imperia, and his ghost has now emerged from the underworld to seek revenge. Revenge promises the ghost of Andrea that he will witness his killer, Prince Balthazar, killed by Bel-Imperia. These two characters remain on stage throughout the play.

At the Spanish court, a general explains that during the battle, Balthazar was defeated in single combat by Horatio and taken prisoner. This ensured Spain's victory, and Portugal has agreed to pay Spain tribute. Balthazar is treated leniently, being merely detained in Spain as the guest of Lorenzo.

At the Portuguese court, the viceroy of Portugal is deceived by Villuppo into believing Balthazar is dead.

Back in Spain, Horatio tells Bel-Imperia of the circumstances of Andrea's death, and she transfers her affections from Andrea to Horatio, who was Andrea's friend. She also vows to have vengeance on Balthazar. Balthazar, encouraged by Lorenzo, declares his love for Bel-Imperia, but she rebuffs him.

The king of Spain holds a banquet, attended by the Portuguese ambassador, to celebrate the new alliance between the two countries. The ghost of Andrea complains to Revenge at seeing Balthazar so well received at the Spanish court. Revenge tells him that friendship will soon turn into enmity.

Act 2

Lorenzo, trying to advance Balthazar's cause with Bel-Imperia, gets her servant Pedringano to admit that she is in love with Horatio, because he has seen letters she sent to him. Lorenzo promises Balthazar that he will get rid of Horatio, leaving Balthazar free to win Bel-Imperia's love. In scene 2, Balthazar and Lorenzo, helped by Pedringano, spy on Bel-Imperia as she and Horatio discuss their love for each other. The new lovers arrange to meet in secret at night, in a garden on Horatio's father's land, where they will not be disturbed.

After a scene in which the duke of Castile agrees to the marriage of his daughter to Balthazar, Lorenzo and Balthazar, informed by Pedringano, surprise Horatio and Bel-Imperia at their secret meeting. They hang and stab Horatio and abduct Bel-Imperia. The disturbance arouses Hieronimo from his bed, and Hieronimo cuts down Horatio and laments his murder. Isabella, his wife, joins him, and he vows revenge. Meanwhile, the ghost of Andrea is again irritated, because he has seen his friend Horatio rather than his enemy Balthazar killed. Revenge replies that he only has to wait, and he will see Balthazar brought low.

Act 3

At the Portuguese court, Alexandro is about to be put to death when the ambassador arrives with the news that Balthazar is alive. The viceroy releases Alexandro and condemns Villuppo to death because of his false claims that Balthazar was dead.

In Spain, Hieronimo, mourning for his son, receives a letter from Bel-Imperia in which she tells him that Horatio was murdered by Lorenzo and Balthazar. She calls on him to take his revenge. Hieronimo, suspicious that the letter may be a trick, resolves to investigate before he takes action. After Hieronimo talks with Lorenzo, Lorenzo becomes suspicious that Hieronimo may know something about the murder. He fears that Balthazar's servant, Serberine, may have said something to him. Lorenzo pays Pedringano to kill Serberine, but after Pedringano shoots Serberine, he is apprehended by three constables, who take him to Hieronimo. Lorenzo then arranges for Pedringano to be executed, while falsely telling him that a pardon already enacted will be revealed at the last minute (thus buying Pedringano's silence). The scheme goes wrong when the hangman shows Hieronimo a letter he has found on the dead Pedringano's clothing that confirms that Lorenzo and Balthazar killed Horatio. Hieronimo resolves to go to the king and seek justice. In the meantime, Isabella goes mad in her grief over her dead son, and Bel-Imperia, who is being kept in seclusion by Lorenzo, bemoans the fact that Hieronimo has not yet avenged Horatio's death.

Lorenzo sends for Bel-Imperia, who rails at him for abducting her. Lorenzo explains that he killed Horatio to protect her honor, since they had met in secret. He reminds her of how her reputation suffered because of her clandestine love affair with Andrea. He also explains that he abducted her lest the king should have found her there. He kept her in seclusion because he wanted to spare her the anger of their father, who is angry at Andrea's death. Balthazar again presses his claim to her love, but Bel-Imperia remains unresponsive.

Meanwhile, the grief-stricken Hieronimo contemplates suicide but decides against it, since if he dies there will be no one to avenge Horatio. Meanwhile, the king, the duke of Castile and the Portuguese ambassador agree on the marriage of Balthazar and Bel-Imperia. Hieronimo bursts in, calling for justice, but after he is restrained and ushered away, Lorenzo tries to convince the king that Hieronimo is not only mad but also wants for himself the ransom paid by Portugal for Balthazar.

Hieronimo forms a plan for vengeance, but waits until the best time to execute it. Meanwhile, he pretends he knows nothing of the guilt of Lorenzo and Balthazar. However, the grief of a man named Bazulto for his murdered son causes Hieronimo to reproach himself for delaying his revenge.

The viceroy arrives for the wedding, and Castile reproaches his son Lorenzo for obstructing Hieronimo's access to the king. When Hieronimo enters, summoned by Castile, Hieronimo pretends to be reconciled with Lorenzo. The act concludes with the ghost of Andrea again calling for revenge. Revenge reassures him, in the process explaining to Andrea the meaning of a "dumb show" (mimed performance) they have just witnessed.

Act 4

Bel-Imperia reproaches Hieronimo for failing to avenge Horatio and tells him that if he does not act, she will carry out her revenge herself. Hieronimo reassures her that he has a plan, and asks her to join with him. Lorenzo and Balthazar enter and ask Hieronimo to devise some entertainment for the Portuguese ambassador. Hieronimo produces a tragic play that he wrote when he was young. He assigns them all parts. Balthazar is to play Soliman the Turkish Emperor who pursues a woman, Perseda (played by Bel-Imperia), who kills him after one of Soliman's men (played by Hieronimo) kills her husband, Erastus (played by Lorenzo).

Isabella, believing that Hieronimo has abdicated his revenge, curses the garden where Horatio was murdered, and then kills herself.

The play is acted in front of the Spanish king, the viceroy of Portugal, and other members of the court. At the appropriate moment in the plot, Hieronimo stabs Erastus (Lorenzo). Bel-Imperia stabs Soliman (Balthazar) and then stabs herself. The on-stage audience does not realize the deaths are real, not feigned. Then Hieronimo produces the body of Horatio and explains how Horatio was murdered, and that the deaths of Balthazar and Lorenzo are real, designed by him. Bel-Imperia he had intended to spare, but she took it upon herself to commit suicide. Hieronimo then tries to hang himself. He is restrained, and the king demands that he explain himself fully. Hieronimo refuses to explain what role Bel-Imperia had in the plot, and bites out his tongue rather than speak. A pen is brought for him to write down an explanation. Hieronimo indicates he needs a knife to mend the pen, but when the knife is brought, he stabs the duke of Castile and himself.

In the final scene, the ghost of Andrea is pleased by what he has witnessed. He looks forward to welcoming Horatio, Bel-Imperia, Isabella and Hieronimo in pleasant circumstances. Revenge tells him that he can hurl his enemies to the deepest hell, and Andrea picks out the punishments for them that best please him.

Characters

Alexandro

Alexandro is a noble in the Portuguese court. He is falsely accused by Villuppo of accidentally causing the death of Balthazar in battle. He is condemned to death by the viceroy, but the truth eventually comes out, and Alexandro is released.

Ambassador of Portugal

The ambassador of Portugal acts as a liaison between the courts of Spain and Portugal.

Balthazar

Balthazar, the prince of Portugal, kills Don Andrea in battle, and thus becomes the object of the desire for revenge exhibited by Andrea's ghost. Balthazar falls in love with Bel-Imperia, angering the ghost still further, since Andrea was Bel-Imperia's lover. Balthazar is frustrated by Bel-Imperia's lack of affection for him, and he participates in the murder of Horatio, whom Bel-Imperia loves, in order to remove his rival. In the play-within-the-play, Balthazar plays the role of Soliman, the sultan of Turkey. He is stabbed to death by Bel-Imperia.

Bel-Imperia

Bel-Imperia is the daughter of Don Ciprian, the duke of Castile, and the brother of Lorenzo. She was Don Andrea's lover before he was killed in battle by Balthazar. After Andrea's death, Bel-Imperia falls in love with Horatio. She hates Balthazar, since he was the cause of her lover's death. Bel-Imperia writes a letter to Hieronimo, informing him of who killed Horatio, and she expects him to carry out his revenge against the murderers. In the play-within-the-play, Bel-Imperia plays Perseda. She kills the character Soliman, played by Balthazar, and then stabs herself to death, even though her suicide is not called for in the role she is playing.

Christophill

Christophill is Lorenzo's servant.

Don Ciprian

Don Ciprian, duke of Castile, is the brother of the king of Spain, and father of Lorenzo and Bel-Imperia. He plays little part in the main action, although he does rebuke Lorenzo for thwarting Hieronimo's access to the king. Don Ciprian then effects what he believes to be a reconciliation between the two. Although the duke is innocent of any involvement in the death of Horatio, Hieronimo kills him after the play-within-the-play is over.

Duke of Castile

See Don Ciprian

Ghost of Don Andrea

Andrea was a Spanish courtier who was in love with Bel-Imperia. He was killed in battle by Balthazar, and his ghost now demands revenge against Balthazar. The ghost and the personified figure of Revenge emerge from the underworld and watch all the events of the play unfold at the Spanish court.

Hieronimo

Hieronimo is the knight marshal of Spain and the father of Horatio. Filled with grief at Horatio's murder, Heironimo vows to take revenge on his son's killers. But before he acts, he wants to make sure he knows for certain the identities of the guilty men. He does not take Bel-Imperia's word for it when she writes him a letter telling him what happened. Hieronimo decides to watch and wait, and not to betray his suspicions to anyone. He is finally convinced of the guilt of Lorenzo and Balthazar when an incriminating letter is found on the body of the hanged Pedringano. But still Hieronimo is frustrated; he cannot understand why heaven does not hear his call for justice and vengeance. He goes almost mad with grief, and contemplates, but ultimately rejects, suicide. Hieronimo goes to the king demanding justice, but

Lorenzo interrupts him before he can explain himself. Finally, Hieronimo devises a form of revenge by means of a performance of a tragic play he wrote when he was young. He ensures that the two guilty men play characters who are killed. During the course of the play, Hieronimo really kills Lorenzo and ensures that Balthazar is killed by Bel-Imperia. When the play ends, Hieronimo brings out the dead body of Horatio and explains himself to the shocked audience. He tries to hang himself, then bites out his tongue rather than divulge the full story to the king. He stabs the duke of Castile and then stabs himself.

Don Horatio

Don Horatio is the son of Hieronimo and a friend of Andrea's. Horatio defeats Balthazar in single combat during the battle between the Spanish and Portuguese armies. He then takes the place of the dead Andrea in Bel-Imperia's affections. Horatio is killed by Lorenzo and Balthazar because he is an obstacle to the marriage between Balthazar and Bel-Imperia.

Isabella

Isabella is Hieronimo's wife. Grief-stricken over the murder of her son Horatio, and the delay in exacting revenge against his killer, she eventually goes mad and commits suicide.

King of Spain

The king of Spain is an honorable man. Although he celebrates the Spanish victory over Portugal, he does not behave vindictively towards the defeated foe. He treats Balthazar, the captured prince, generously, and welcomes Balthazar's proposed marriage to Bel-Imperia, since this will cement an alliance between Spain and Portugal.

Lorenzo

Lorenzo is the son of the duke of Castile, and Bel-Imperia's brother. He is an evil, scheming character who will stop at nothing to ensure that Bel-Imperia elevates her status by marrying Balthazar. He plans and takes part in the murder of Horatio, and then arranges for two of his accomplices, Pedringano and Serberine, to be killed. Lorenzo plays the character of Erastus in the play-within-the-play. He is killed by Hieronimo.

Pedringano

Pedringano is a servant of Bel-Imperia. Lorenzo uses him to advance his scheme against Horatio, and also persuades him to kill Serberine. Pedringano is then arrested, and Lorenzo buys his silence by promising him a pardon. But Lorenzo double-crosses him, and Pedringano is hanged.

Don Pedro

Don Pedro is the brother of the viceroy of Portugal.

Revenge

Revenge is the personified abstraction of the desire of Don Andrea to be revenged on Balthazar. When Don Andrea's ghost becomes frustrated at the events he witnesses, which do not seem to be leading in the direction he wants, Revenge promises him that revenge will come; all the ghost must do is wait.

Serberine

Serberine is a servant of Balthazar who is killed by Pedringano on the instructions of Lorenzo.

Viceroy of Portugal

The viceroy of Portugal is deceived by Villuppo into believing that his son Balthazar was killed in battle. When he finds out that he has been deceived, the viceroy condemns Villuppo to death. The viceroy mends relations with Spain by agreeing to pay tribute. He also consents to the proposed marriage between Balthazar and Bel-Imperia. The viceroy is a spectator at the play during which his son is killed.

Villuppo

Villuppo is a Portuguese nobleman who gives

the Viceroy false information about the fate of Balthazar. He insists that the Prince was killed in battle, even though he knows this is not true. When his lie is discovered, Villuppo is put to death.

Themes

Justice and Revenge

The single theme of the play is revenge. The theme appears in many different aspects of the plot, with varying degrees of moral justification. It is introduced at the very beginning, when the ghost of Andrea wants revenge on Balthazar for having killed him in battle, although there is nothing the ghost can directly do to bring it about.

The next character who wants revenge is Bel-Imperia, whose desired victim is also Balthazar, since he killed her lover, Andrea. Initially, she plans to use Horatio as her means of vengeance, and when Horatio is murdered, she has a double motive for revenge.

The third example of the desire for revenge is Balthazar, who wants revenge on Horatio for taking him prisoner in battle and being an obstacle to Balthazar's attempt to win Bel-Imperia.

The last and most important example of the revenge theme is Hieronimo, who seeks revenge for the slaying of his son, Horatio. Hieronimo's wife, Isabella, shares his desire.

Even though Horatio's murder does not occur until late in the second act, Hieronimo's revenge is the main focus of the play, as it is he who has suffered the greatest wrong. It might be argued, for example, that Andrea has little cause to seek revenge on Balthazar, since they met on the battlefield in a fair fight. But Hieronimo has what anyone might regard as just cause. Also, the audience has witnessed the murder of Horatio directly—in contrast, the audience has only been told about the death of Andrea—which gives this aspect of the plot more emotional force.

Once the revenge plot is in place, the question becomes how it is to take place. Whose responsibility is it to exact revenge? Hieronimo's first thought is that he will do it himself. But Isabella introduces the idea that "the heavens are just" and that time will bring the villains to light, and, presumably, to punishment.

Not long after this, in act 3, scene 2, Hieronimo, frustrated at not knowing the identity of the murderer, severely questions the notion of cosmic justice. In lines 9–11, he appeals directly to the "sacred heavens," saying that if the murder

> Shall unrevealed and unrevengéd pass,
> How should we term your dealings to be just,
> If you unjustly deal with those that in your justice trust?

Immediately after this appeal, Hieronimo finds the letter from Bel-Imperia, informing him that the murderers are Balthazar and Lorenzo—which suggests that the wheels of cosmic justice are in fact responsive to his plight. However, Hieronimo is beginning to believe that he must carry out the vengeance himself. But he is very concerned about the idea of justice. He does not want to strike until he is certain of the guilt of those whom he suspects. When Hieronimo finally comes upon incontrovertible proof of the identity of the murderers, he thanks heaven because he believes it is the gods who have refused to let the murder go unpunished.

Still concerned with justice and how to execute it, Hieronimo resolves to take his case to the king and seek secular justice. It is only the intervention of Lorenzo that stops him explaining the whole story to the king. With the failure of this strategy, and after briefly considering the Christian idea that revenge should be left to God, Hieronimo decides to take vengeance into his own hands. Even then, he believes that his solution to the problem is in fact "wrought by the heavens." Most modern readers feel that Hieronimo goes too far, since he also kills the duke of Castile. The duke is innocent of any wrongdoing; he is killed simply because he is Lorenzo's father.

This excess on the part of Hieronimo makes it difficult to argue that he is merely the agent of divine justice. It appears that he has stepped over the line that divides a just avenger from a murderer and a villain. His final actions also suggest that any human attempt to enact justice is fraught with danger and prone to error. An example of the fallibility of human justice occurs in the trial and execution of Pedringano. Pedringano may deserve his fate, but the legal process he goes through fails entirely to establish the fact that he was acting on the orders of Lorenzo, who, at least in this instance, escapes punishment.

Style

Dramatic Irony

The play consistently employs dramatic irony, a situation in which one or more characters act without full knowledge of the facts, but those facts are known by the audience. For example, in act 1, scene 3, the viceroy of Portugal mourns the son he believes to be dead, but the audience knows Balthazar is alive. In act 2, scene 2, when Bel-Imperia and Horatio declare their love for each other, the audience knows that a plot is already in motion to destroy their love. Indeed, in that same scene Lorenzo and Balthazar, unseen watchers, state explicitly what awaits the two lovers. The audience is also aware that after Pedringano has murdered Serberine, the pardon Pedrigano so confidently expects, and on which he bases his words and actions, does not exist.

There is also a dramatic irony that frames the entire play, since on several occasions, the figure of Revenge tells the ghost of Andrea what the outcome will be. The audience is not allowed to forget this, since those two characters remain on stage throughout the play. The effect of this dramatic irony is to show that, even while the characters are plotting to avoid or hasten certain events, their fate is already determined, though unknown to them. The characters may think they are in control of their situation, as Lorenzo and Balthazar do, but they cannot escape the destiny that is marked out for them.

Stichomythia

The play frequently employs a rhetorical device known as stichomythia, which Kyd derived from Seneca, the Roman writer of tragedies. Stichomythia is a quick-fire dialogue between two or more characters, in which each character gives a one-line response. The responses often echo the words of the previous line. An example occurs in act 2, scene 3, lines 24–30 in the dialogue between Bel-Imperia, Balthazar and Horatio:

> BEL-IMPERIA: Why stands Horatio speechless all this while?
>
> HORATIO: The less I speak, the more I meditate. BEL-IMPERIA: But whereon dost thou chiefly meditate?
>
> HORATIO: On dangers past, and pleasures to ensue.
>
> BALTHAZAR: On pleasures past, and dangers to ensue.
>
> BEL-IMPERIA: What dangers and what pleasures dost thou mean?
>
> HORATIO: Dangers of war and pleasures of our love.

Anaphora

Another frequent device is anaphora, the repetition of a word or words at the beginning of each line of verse, as in Lorenzo's speech in act 2, scene 1:

'In time the savage bull sustains the yoke,
In time all haggard hawks will stoop to lure,
In time small wedges cleave the hardest oak,
In time the flint is pierced with softest shower—'

Topics for Further Study

- Research the English attitude towards Spain in Elizabethan times. Analyze ways in which this attitude sheds light on the play.

- Does Hieronimo retain the sympathy of the audience until the end of the play, or does he become a villain too? Does his madness cloud his judgment?

- Research the work and influence of the sixteenth century political philosopher, Niccolo Machiavelli. In what sense might Lorenzo be considered a Machiavellian figure?

- What is the difference between revenge and justice? Are the two concepts sometimes merged? Can revenge ever be justified?

Alliteration

Alliteration, the repetition of initial consonants, is another frequently used device. It occurs, for example, in Hieronimo's speech at the beginning of act 3, scene 7, where he questions where he can run to with his woes, "woes whose weight hath wearied the earth?" The blustering winds, he continues, have "Made mountains marsh with spring-tides of my tears, / And broken through the brazen gates of hell."

The Revenge Play

After Kyd had shown the way with *The Spanish Tragedy*, the revenge play became extremely popular on the Elizabethan stage. John Marston's *Antonio's Revenge,* Christopher Marlowe's *The Jew of Malta,* and Shakespeare's *Titus Andronicus* and *Hamlet* are some of the most outstanding plays of this type.

The revenge play was adapted from the work of the Roman playwright Seneca (4 B.C. to A.D. 65). Seneca wrote nine tragedies, based on Greek models, but his plays were meant to be recited rather than performed on a stage. They consisted mainly of long speeches, and action was described rather than presented directly. Seneca's theme was revenge and retribution, and his subject matter was lurid; his plays feature crimes such as murder, incest, and adultery, and there is much blood, mutilation, and carnage. Ghosts appear frequently, and the plays end in a horrible catastrophe. Seneca emphasized that man was helpless to avert his tragic fate, but if he could meet it with stoic resolve he would in a sense remain undefeated.

Seneca's plays held great appeal all across Renaissance Europe. In England, the first original English tragedy based on Seneca's model was *Gorboduc,* by Thomas Sackville and Thomas

Norton, which was first performed in 1562. During the 1560s, many translations of Seneca's plays, and original plays based on Seneca, were written by university playwrights. Another Senecan revival occurred during the 1580s, in the work not only of Kyd but also of George Peele.

The Senecan basis of *The Spanish Tragedy* can be seen in Kyd's theme of murder and revenge, the presence of a ghost, and a bloody trail of events. At one point, Hieronimo even carries a copy of Seneca's play *Agamemnon* in his hand and quotes from it. But Kyd and his contemporaries made one important change to the Senecan tradition. In *The Spanish Tragedy*, typical Senecan horrors (the hanging and stabbing of Horatio, and Hieronimo's self-mutilation, for example) are shown directly on stage rather than being merely reported by a messenger. This appeared to satisfy the more crude instincts of an Elizabethan audience that regularly enjoyed such violent spectacles as public hangings and whippings, bear-baiting and the like. It also made for an exciting, action-packed spectacle.

The Elizabethan enthusiasm for revenge plays was for the most part a dramatic interest only. Although in these types of plays, revenge is presented as an honorable, even sacred duty (Hamlet, for example, never doubts his duty to avenge his murdered father), Elizabethan society did not sanction acts of private revenge. A murder committed to avenge the murder of a close relative was treated no differently in Elizabethan law than any other murder. The punishment for an avenger was the same as for the original murderer.

However, despite the insistence by the authorities, secular as well as religious, on the rule of law, family feuds did take place in Elizabethan England, and almost always took the form of the duel. There were other instances as well in which revenge, although officially condemned, might be countenanced. If a known murderer could not be brought to justice because of lack of evidence that could be presented in court, or if a man's high position in society enabled him to put himself above the law, the average Elizabethan might have had some sympathy and tolerance for an act of private revenge.

The Spanish Tragedy was extremely popular during the last decade of the sixteenth century and was performed well into the seventeenth century. It was also successful as a printed book, with six editions printed between 1602 and 1633. According to Thomas W. Ross, in his edition of the play, it was "the most prodigious success of any drama produced and printed between 1580 and 1642," dates that would include all of Shakespeare's works. Translations of the play were performed in Europe; a performance was recorded in Frankfurt in 1601. The play was so well known in England that certain passages, such as Hieronimo's extravagant expressions of grief and Andrea's speech in the prologue, were subject to many parodies by other playwrights, who must have known that their audiences would recognize the allusions to the earlier play.

However, *The Spanish Tragedy* has not been performed by professional companies since 1642, and was largely forgotten until historians of drama discovered its importance in the early twentieth century. They realized that the play was a seminal work that revealed much about the development of tragedy, and especially revenge tragedy, in Elizabethan England.

Modern scholars have claimed that *The Spanish Tragedy* has more than mere historical interest. J. R. Mulryne, in his introduction to the New Mermaid edition of the play, notes that it is "remarkable for the astonishingly deft and complete way in which Kyd has transmuted his theme into drama, by way of the intricate tactics of his play's structure." Mulryne claimed that a professional production would show that the play "deserve[s] its place as one of the first important English tragedies." Philip Edwards, in *Thomas Kyd and Early Elizabethan Tragedy,* declared that in conception, although not in execution, *The Spanish Tragedy* was "more original, and greater, than [Shakespeare's] *Richard III.* It is one of those rare works in which a minor writer, in a strange inspiration, shapes the future by producing something quite new."

Compare & Contrast

- **1580s:** Spain is the leading world power. In 1588, the English fleet defeats the Spanish Armada, and so prevents an invasion by Catholic Spain of Protestant England.

  Today: Spain and Britain are mid-level European powers. Both are members of NATO and the European Union.

- **1580s:** Elizabethan authors do not own the copyright to their work; they are poorly paid by the theater companies to which they sell their work, and they do not receive royalties from the publisher. Plays are often published anonymously, and pirated or corrupt editions appear, sometimes based on an actor's memory of the script or a copy made by a spectator during a performance.

Today: Strict copyright laws define ownership of a literary work, and legally enforceable contracts define the amount of royalties an author receives. Plagiarism or infringement of copyright is illegal and offenders may be prosecuted.

- **1580s:** London is the largest city in Europe, with a population of over 100,000. Many foreigners come to live in the city, taking advantage of lenient immigration laws and the willingness of employers to hire aliens. Whenever unemployment rises, Londoners tend to blame the presence of foreigners.

Today: With a population of 7,172,036, London remains one of the most populous cities in Europe, along with Moscow, Istanbul, and Paris. Patterns of immigration have changed over the centuries, and London is now a multi-cultural, multi-ethnic city. Ten percent of the population is Indian, Bangladeshi, or Pakistani; 5 percent is African, and 5 percent come from the Caribbean.

What Do I Read Next?

- The plays collected in *Four Revenge Tragedies: "The Spanish Tragedy," "The Revenger's Tragedy," "The Revenge of Bussy D'Ambois," and "The Atheist's Tragedy"* (Oxford World's Classics, 2000), edited by Katharine Eisaman Maus, show how the Elizabethan revenge tragedy was treated by dramatists such as George Chapman (*Revenge of Bussy D'Ambois*), Cyril Tourneur (*The Atheist's Tragedy*) and the author of the anonymous *The Revenger's Tragedy* (which is sometimes ascribed to Tourneur or Thomas Middleton).

- M. C. Bradbrook's *Themes and Conventions of Elizabethan Tragedy* (2d ed., 1980) deals with the conventions which gave Elizabethan drama its special character. Bradbrook also analyzes individual plays by Marlowe, Tourneur, Middleton, and John Webster. There are many allusions to Kyd and to Shakespeare.

- *English Renaissance Drama: A Norton Anthology* (2002), edited by David M. Bevington, Lars Engle, Katharine Eisaman Maus, and Eric Rasmussen, is an extensive collection of twenty-seven plays written in Elizabethan and Jacobean England. Playwrights represented include Marlowe, Middleton, Webster, and Ben Jonson.

- *A New History of Early English Drama* (1998), by John D. Cox and David Scott Kastan, is an innovative collection of twenty-six essays on early modern English drama, up to 1642. The essays cover such topics as the conditions under which plays were written, produced and disseminated. The emphasis is not on individual authors but on the place of the stage in the wider society, and how it was impacted by religious, civic and other cultural factors.

Sources

Bowers, Fredson Thayer, *Elizabethan Revenge Tragedy, 1587–1642,* Princeton University Press, 1940, pp. 3–100.

Broude, Ronald, "Time, Truth, and Right in *The Spanish Tragedy,*" in *Studies in Philology,* Vol. 68, 1971, p. 131.

Burrows, Ken C., "The Dramatic and Structural Significance of the Portuguese Sub-plot in *The Spanish Tragedy,*" in *Renaissance Papers,* Fall 1969, p. 30.

Edwards, Philip, *Thomas Kyd and Early Elizabethan Tragedy,* Longmans, 1966, p. 6.

——, "Thrusting Elysium into Hell: The Originality of *The Spanish Tragedy,*" in *The Elizabethan Theatre XI,* edited by A. L. Magnusson and C. E. McGee, P. D. Meany, 1985, pp. 123, 131–32.

Erne, Lukas, *Beyond "The Spanish Tragedy": A Study of the Works of Thomas Kyd,* Manchester University Press, 2001, pp. 110–11.

Hunter, G. K. "Ironies of Justice in *The Spanish Tragedy,*" in *Dramatic Identities and Cultural Tradition: Studies in Shakespeare and His Contemporaries,* Barnes & Noble, 1978, p. 220; originally published in *Renaissance Drama,* Vol. 8, 1965.

Justice, Steven, "Spain, Tragedy, and *The Spanish*

Tragedy," in *Studies in English Literature,* Vol. 25, 1985, p. 274.

Kyd, Thomas, *The Spanish Tragedy,* edited by J. R. Mulryne, New Mermaid ed., Hill and Wang, 1970.

——, *The Spanish Tragedy,* edited by Thomas W. Ross, University of California Press, 1968.

Murray, Peter B. *Thomas Kyd,* Twayne Publishers, 1969, pp. 54, 127.

Shakespeare, William, *Hamlet,* edited by Harold Jenkins, Arden Shakespeare ed., Methuen, 1982.

Stockholder, Kay, "'Yet Can He Write': Reading the Silences in *The Spanish Tragedy,"* in *American Imago,* Vol. 47, No. 2, Summer 1990, p. 101.

Wiatt, William H., "The Dramatic Function of the Alexandro-Villuppo Episode in *The Spanish Tragedy,"* in *Notes and Queries,* n.s., Vol. 5, 1958, pp. 327–28.

Further Reading

Clemen, Wolfgang, *English Tragedy before Shakespeare,* Methuen, 1961, pp. 100–12.

> This is an analysis of the long set speeches in *The Spanish Tragedy.* Clemen shows Kyd's originality in integrating these speeches with the structure of the plot and in presenting them in a more dramatic fashion than their Senecan models.

Freeman, Arthur, *Thomas Kyd: Facts and Problems,* Clarendon Press, 1967.

> This is the most comprehensive account of Kyd's life and works. It includes detailed discussions of the date and sources of *The Spanish Tragedy,* as well as its style, structure, stage history, parodies, textual additions, and critical reception.

Harbage, Alfred, "Intrigue in Elizabethan Tragedy," in *Essays on Shakespeare and Elizabethan Drama, in Honor of Hardin Craig,* edited by Richard Hosley, University of Missouri Press, 1962, pp. 37–44.

> Harbage argues that one of Kyd's distinctive and influential achievements was his introduction

into tragedy of the element of intrigue, in which the action is complicated. In doing this, Kyd also employs comic methods, thus creating a kind of "comitragedy."

Johnson, S. F., "*The Spanish Tragedy,* or Babylon Revisited," in *Essays on Shakespeare and Elizabethan Drama, in Honor of Hardin Craig,* edited by Richard Hosley, University of Missouri Press, 1962, pp. 23–36.

Johnson argues that in the play, Spain is equated with the Biblical Babylon, which God promises to destroy. Hieronimo's vengeance is therefore just, since it brings down the king of Spain, whom many English Protestants regarded as being in league with the Antichrist, the pope.

Murray, Peter B., *Thomas Kyd,* Twayne's English Authors Series, No. 88, Twayne, 1969.

Murray sketches the literary and historical background of the play and then analyzes it scene by scene in terms of the development of action, character and theme. The final chapter considers the play's relation to the tragedies that followed it, with attention to the additions to Kyd's play that were published in 1602. Murray also includes a chronology and an annotated bibliography.

Lightning Source UK Ltd.
Milton Keynes UK
UKHW02f0632190918
329155UK00012B/1127/P